Growing Marijuana Hydroponically

Tina Wright
Hans

Ronin Publishing, Inc.
Oakland, CA
roninpub.com

GROWING MARIJUANA HYDROPONICALLY
ISBN: 0-914171-54-2
ISBN:978-0-914171-54-6

Copyright 2000 by Tina Wright
Copyright: 2011 by Beverly A. Potter

Published by:
RONIN PUBLISHING, INC.
Post Office Box 22900
Oakland CA 94609
roninpub.com

Editors: Barry Katzmann, Phillip Smith
Cover design: Judy July, Generic

Distributed by Publishers Group West/Perseus
Library of Congress Card Number: 00-190009

This book is dedicated
to four beautiful flowers.

Monaca
Leann
Emily
Erin

It's my pleasure in life
to watch you grow and bloom.

I love you all.

Notice To Reader

The material in this book is for adults only. Parents, guardians and other adults should exercise appropriate control to keep this book out of the hands of minors.

This book is a reference work made available for educational, informational, archival, entertainment and any other purposes protected by the First Amendment of the Constitution of the United States of America.

CAUTION: Growing and possessing marijuana is illegal under federal laws. The author and publisher do not advocate breaking the law. Persons considering implementing procedures described herein should consult with an attorney before doing so.

The author and publisher do not accept liability for any actions any person may have taken after reading this book. The author and publisher do, however, encourage readers to support efforts to legalize marijuana and its cultivation.

Table of Contents

Preface

The information in this book covers beginning to advanced methods and concepts, providing a step-by-step, day-by-day account of the creation of a successful indoor hydroponic marijuana garden.

We have adapted the simple Ebb and Flow Method into the Sea of Green Perpetual Harvest process, wherein hydroponic techniques are refined a few steps further than in previous methods to create a truly unique procedure. We have also adapted the method to a "cottage" approach to hydroponic cultivation, in which any size grow area can be created through a combination of high-tech concepts and low-tech materials.

The Sea of Green Perpetual Harvest process is the simplest, quickest method for growing marijuana hydroponically. It reduces the time required to produce a bud of marijuana, because the process eliminates the need to grow an entire plant. Instead, only buds are grown. Clones are taken from a mother plant and grown until they are about 12 inches long. The clones are then placed into bloom and the end result is a single-stalk bud or single-stalk bush. Using the Sea of Green Perpetual Harvest method allows for precise control of the harvest. Crop harvesting can be rotated once a week, every two weeks, or even once a day. The timing between each harvest can be individualized.

Marijuana brings pleasure to a multitude of people by inducing euphoria while serving other beneficial purposes. It is as soft as cotton and more durable when processed into material for clothing. It is strong, which is why hemp has been used in rope manufacture for years.

Most marijuana smokers prefer plants that have been organically grown, because they do not want marijuana that is contaminated by the residual chemicals that can remain in hydroponically grown plants after harvest. This problem is solved through the wick method, which allows the chemicals present in the plant to be depleted during the two to three weeks before harvest, thereby leaving only a small proportion of the chemicals in the plant fiber. The result is the much-sought-after quality found in superior, high-grade marijuana: organic, chemical-free, sweet-tasting smoke.

Introduction

Hydroponics is the practice of cultivating plants in a nutrient solution instead of in soil. *Hydro* comes from the Greek word for *water* and *ponics* is taken from the word *geoponics,* which refers to the study or science of agriculture.

There are several different hydroponic techniques. The two most common methods of hydroponic growing are the Ebb and Flow (E&F) method and the Nutrient Film/Flow Technique (NFT). Of the two methods, E&F is the easiest and most forgiving.

Most hydroponic techniques incorporate a *medium,* or stratum, of artificial soil. This is usually an inert substance that retains moisture and serves as a holding stratum, or layer of material, for the root system of each plant to grasp. As the roots of the plants grow through the medium, they are constantly supplied with nutrient-laden water. The periodic flooding of roots creates periods between watering in which the plants are exposed to more oxygen, facilitating a rapid use of the nutrients, resulting in faster growth.

Plants are like people. They require simple, basic things to thrive. They need water, air, light, nutrients, a medium in which to grow and a comfortable temperature. In hydroponic cultivation, each of these basic needs are properly regulated to adequately serve the plants. Like all living things, plants follow certain cycles. The art of growing lies in the manipulation of the cycles to the advantage of the hydroponic garden, which is a conditioned and precision-controlled environment.

The unknown grower.

This book begins by detailing the major considerations in starting hydroponic marijuana gardens. The first step is determining the location of the growing area. A decision is then made about the size and number of plants to be grown before the grow area is prepared. Next, equipment is purchased and tested for several days to confirm that it is completely functional. Environmental variables, such as exhaust, temperature control, light and so forth are checked to make sure they are perfectly adjusted.

The combination of the Sea of Green Perpetual Harvest hydroponic wick method with the cottage approach is called the *Hans Process*. It is a simple, unique growing technique. Day-to-day, week-by-week descriptions of the Hans beginning hydroponic garden technique are included in later chapters.

Hydroponic growing is rewarding and fun and yields "mega-buds" faster than is possible with most soil methods. On the other hand, hydroponic gardening is less forgiving than soil gardening, because it is more difficult to control the nutrient level of a hydroponic garden than that of a soil-based one. When growing hydroponically, mistakes are usually not noticed until the damage to the plants has progressed to a serious level.

**Lush plant grown hydroponically is
almost ready to harvest.**

Chapter 1

How Plants Grow

Imagine an entire world created artificially. The light source is a fluorescent or high intensity discharge (HID). Air and wind are created by fans. Instead of soil, nutrient-filled humus comes from a bottle and life-giving rain is supplied at controlled intervals. Simulation of an ideal environment and fine-tuning of the results create the perfect indoor conditions for growing marijuana.

Mere knowledge of the secrets of environmental control is not sufficient to grow a successful indoor marijuana crop. Also needed is an understanding of the physical functioning of the marijuana plant itself: how it works, why it works and in what ways it works. Total, conscious control of the growing environment provides the maximum potential for a healthy, potent crop of plants.

Germination

In nature, the proper combination of moisture, oxygen and temperature must be present.

In an indoor grow room, these and other conditions must be maintained exactly. If they are not, the plants will be less productive and have a greater risk of dying.

When conditions are favorable in the outdoors, a seed is cast upon the ground and will grow. If all the requirements for life are in abundance, then life may begin.

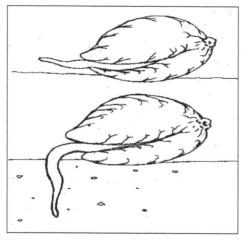

A horn-shaped root tip emerges from a seed and grows in a downward direction.

Moisture softens the seed shell so that the embryo within swells, creating pressure on the seeds.

Germination begins with the splitting of the shell casing, followed by the emergence of a tiny white horn-shaped root tip.

Roots

The new root grows in a downward direction as it seeks refuge in the soil and elongates into a *taproot*, or main root. As the root grows it develops small, fine hairs and lateral roots. If oxygen is present, the fine root hairs absorb nutrients and water from the soil or growing medium.

As cells in the tip of the root grow deeper into the soil they take on more selective responsibili-

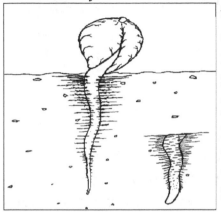

Lateral rootlets extend from the main taproot.

ties and functions, serving as anchors for the plant, storing nutrients and transporting water. After a seed germinates and sends its root downward, a similar reaction takes place in the above-ground parts of the plant. Cellular growth aims upward toward the surface of the soil. As the embryo grows it forces open and casts off the softened shell, resulting in the emergence of two rounded leaves from the seed shell, called the *cotyledon leaves*. As they grow, they respond to light and are joined by a second set that exhibit the familiar serrated appearance of marijuana leaves.

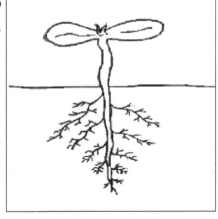

Cotyledon leaves.

Stems

The stem is located be-
tween the lower root and
the upper leaves. Like the
embryo, it is regulated by
growth cells that follow
predetermined patterns.
The stem lengthens as
each new set of leaves is
created on the tip of the

**The root, stem and leaf
of a young plant.**

plant. The point of creation is called a *node*.

As growth progresses, more growing terminals develop. Between the new set of leaves
and the stem of the plant, a lateral branch
grows at each new node. Portions of the stem
between nodes are called *internodes.* They, too,
lengthen in a fashion peculiar to the plant's genetic ability and its environmental conditions.
As the plant gets older, more nodes and lateral
growth are produced. The stem has a variety
of functions, including creating and holding
leaves at proper intervals while transporting
water and food to the rest of the plant.

Leaves

The nutrients and water are partially consumed as they are delivered up the stem to the
top of the plant. As water and nutrients reach
the leaves, they are mixed with carbon diox-

ide (CO_2). With the help of sunlight and chlorophyll, the leaves create carbohydrates and oxygen by a process called *photosynthesis.*

In order for the chlorophyll to be able to do its job properly, the leaves, like the roots and stems, must have an adequate amount of water. The outer and inner parts of the leaves are completely dependent on water, so a certain level of moisture must be present at all times. If a leaf becomes too dry it cannot function properly and will probably die.

The underside of a marijuana leaf is covered with small holes called *stomata* that open and close to regulate the outward flow of moisture, thus protecting the leaves from drying out. In addition, the stomata evacuate excess moisture and

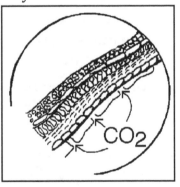

Stomata Bottom of leaf. Stomata allow carbon dioxide to enter plant.

waste products and serve as the portals by which carbon dioxide enters the plant.

If the roots, stem and leaves do not receive proper provisions, there will be a breakdown of related processes, because the plant functions holistically. If one part of the plant ceases to function properly, other interwoven functions break down.

The following chapters explain the conditions required for successful indoor hydroponic growing. The accommodation of necessary life processes, both external and internal, at all stages of the marijuana plant's development must be followed exactly.

Pests

Sooner or later most plants attract some form of pest. Gardeners must always be on the lookout for indications of these intruders: the telltale signs are usually yellowish spots, which are bite marks, on the underside of the leaves. There may also be web- or thread-like substances or yellowish secretions, though most frequently the offending insects themselves are spotted. Casually looking for pests is not sufficient; plants must be checked thoroughly and regularly with a magnifying glass.

Organic pyrethrum, an insecticide made from the dried flower heads of chrysanthemums, can be used when a bug is first sighted. Directions for its use, found on the insecticide's package, must be followed exactly. Generally, it is applied once and then again seven days later, and then another seven-day waiting period must pass before a final application.

Chapter 2

Grow Room Setup

Hydroponic gardens can be set up in many places, including inside houses or in enclosed areas such as garages or sheds. Where grow areas can be set up is limited only by space restrictions and one's imagination.

Generally an outbuilding or an out-of-the-way place in the house is selected. There may be space in a basement, an attic or a spare room. In-house gardens are usually hidden by a false wall covering a door or by simply keeping the door locked and away from prying eyes.

When a location has been determined to be suitable, it is cleared of non-growing items and thoroughly cleaned, after which it is enclosed and hidden if needed. Carpets are removed from the floors, and walls and ceiling are painted with flat white paint.

The Sea of Green Perpetual Harvest process, a specialized, mass-production technique for growing marijuana indoors, requires two different light schedules. Therefore, the growing area is divided into two separate sections: the *cloning area* and the *blooming area.*

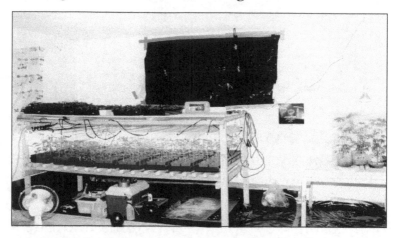

Seedling and cloning area can be part of a larger room (as above) or set up in a closet or other speparate space.

A typical garden is 12 by 8 by 8 feet, housed in a small secluded space like a trailor. This is divided into a typical cloning area of 8 by 5 or 6 feet and blooming area of 8 by 7 or 6 feet. Cloning and blooming areas are usually adjacent to each other, separated by a divider or a sliding door.

Having the two areas side-by-side is nice but not absolutely necessary. When space is limited, the cloning area is sometimes set up in the attic, for example, while the blooming area is put in the basement. For instance, one grower established the cloning area in his house but carried out the blooming process in the homes of two friends. A grow room with adjacent areas is used in this book.

The Cloning Area

The cloning area is kept separate from the blooming area. When the two areas are in the same room, they are divided into separate sections. The cloning area houses everything that requires 18 hours of light each 24-hour period, including the seedlings, clones, pre-bloomers and mamma plants. Light is reduced to 12 hours a day when plants are moved into the blooming area.

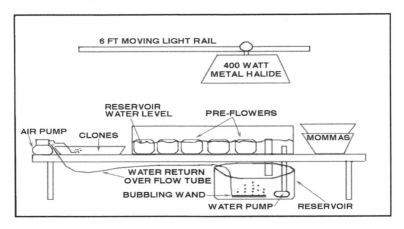

Cloning area setup

The seedlings and clones both use small shallow trays and fluorescent lighting. Pre-bloomers are clones that have rooted, and are planted in larger 6-to-8-inch hydroponic containers. The pre-bloomers sit in a still larger grow bed with its own reservoir. The mammas are placed in wick-method containers. The pre-bloomers and mamma plants are placed under a 400-watt metal halide light bulb that moves on a 6-foot movable rail. Oscillating fans blow only on the pre-bloomers and mammas: fans are never allowed to blow directly on seedlings or clones.

Chapter 3

Air Circulation

Fresh air is essential to growing marijuana. Each growing area needs an air circulation system, whether adjacent or apart, to provide a means for air to enter and exit.

In a hydroponic growing environment, large amounts of water evaporate as air circulates through the water reservoirs and grow beds. Plants also produce water. When air is not re-circulated, it becomes stale and the plants suffer from depletion of vital ingredients such as carbon dioxide.

Exhaust Fan

Exhaust fans are essential. They are oriented so that air is pulled from the growing area, rather than blown into it and out an exhaust portal, because it is easier to pull air

This exhaust fan is baffled so no light escapes.

out of an area than to push it in. Exhaust fans must be equipped with variable speed controls and thermostats.

Better fans come with controls, and controls can be added to less costly, standard fans. Controls permit regulation of air exhaustion rate and room temperature. Timers are used so that exhaustion occurs at a regularly scheduled rate.

Squirrel Cage Fans

Squirrel cage fans are popular. They are small and quiet, and easily connect to six-inch flexible clothes-dryer exhaust hoses. Warm air is evacuated with fans placed on the ceiling. A clothes-dryer exhaust hose is used to vent cooler air through the floor or elsewhere.

Fan performance is measured by its ability to exhaust air, as expressed in cubic feet per minute (cfm). The cubic footage of a room is determined by multiplying the room's width by its length and height.

A fan that can completely exhaust the room in approximately three minutes is used. For example, a room measuring 12 by 8 by 8 feet contains 768 cubic feet, so a 250 cfm exhaust fan will adequately clear the room (250 cfm x 3 minutes = 750 cubic feet).

Fan speed is set to a relatively slow level, so that the air in the room is completely exchanged once every few hours. During and directly after spraying insecticides fans are turned on full blast.

The same is true when the temperature or humidity gets too high. The objective is to maintain a humidity level of 50 percent or lower with a consistent ambient room temperature of 76°F.

Oscillating Fans

Each area needs at least two oscillating fans. One is positioned near the ceiling to blow the warmer air downward to mix it with the lower cooler air. A second fan is placed on the floor and mixes cooler air with the warmer air up near the ceiling. Mixing air maintains a more consistent air temperature.

Fans blowing air gently on the plant tops causes the stems to create cellulose which creates more overall strength in the entire plant and gives it the ability to hold bigger buds upright. The size and strength of the stem is directly related to the total bud size a single plant can support.

Carbon Dioxide

Carbon dioxide (CO_2) is absorbed through the tiny stomata on the underside of each leaf. Carbon dioxide increases the ability of a plant to metabolize available nutrients and water as it engages in photosynthesis.

When carbon dioxide levels reach about 1,500 parts per million (ppm) the plant consumes food rapidly. Sometimes food consumption takes place so quickly that an adequate food supply is depleted. As carbon dioxide is increased in a grow area, the nutrients are also increased. The quantity of carbohydrates and sugars that the plant creates is proportionate to the carbon dioxide it receives.

Outdoors there are 300 to 400 ppm of carbon dioxide concentrated in the atmosphere at any given time. The ppm in a hydroponic garden is generally limited to 1,900, which is the suggested tolerance level for plants.

Compressed tanks of carbon dioxide have regulators that release specific amounts through hoses. The flow of carbon dioxide is directed over the tops of the plants.

Commercial carbon dioxide producers can be used to regulate the carbon dioxide. These machines are safe, simple burners similar to a pilot light encased in a protective enclosure and are often used in winter because of the heat they produce. When maintaining a constant rate is impossible, 900 ppm to 1,500 ppm of CO_2 is approximated as closely as possible.

Plants produce carbon dioxide only when the lights are on or when they are in sunlight. Using carbon dioxide in a dark room is wasteful and should be avoided, because photosynthesis does not occur in the dark.

Temperature

Maintaining a perfect 76°F is desirable but almost impossible in practice. Generally, room temperature is maintained between 72°F and 80°F. A 1,000-watt high-pressure sodium (HPS) lamp raises the temperature of a small room by as much as 10°F. The difference in day and night also produces temperature changes.

Temperature during the artificially created nighttime period is never allowed to drop more than 15°F below the average daily temperature of the indoor grow room. Temperature is never allowed to drop below 60°F or rise above 80°F for more than a brief time. Some growers allow the temperature to reach 80°F briefly when using carbon dioxide because, as noted earlier, it increases plant metabolism so that the extra heat generated is immediately used and damage to the plants is avoided.

Cooling

Air conditioners with thermostats are commonly employed to cool the grow area. They also remove moisture from the air. Air-conditioner air is never permitted to blow directly onto the plants, and clones especially are protected from the direct air stream.

The hottest air in the room is removed by drawing the exhaust from the ceiling. 1,000-watt light fixtures are adapted to fit a six-inch clothes-dryer hose to allow the hot air to be exhausted directly out of the room.

The room temperature can be further regulated by burning the lights during the coolest period, after the sun has set, and having the dark period during the day.

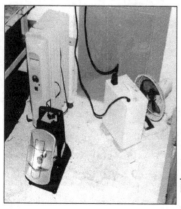

Propane heater (front) and standing oil heater. Fan cools 1000 watt ballast.

Heating

Heating a room draws moisture from the reservoir and plants, which causes a drop in humidity. In the winter a safe propane heater can be used to supply heat as well as carbon dioxide for day time heating. Propane heaters are available with thermostat controls and safety thermal coupling units. Standing oil heaters are used at night.

Covering the walls, ceiling and floors with thick Styrofoam™ helps keep the grow area temperature at a consistent level year-round.

Safety First

Fire is always a risk which is why care is to be taken when selecting all heating equipment, because heating a grow room can be dangerous.

Radiant strip heaters are never placed close to or facing anything that is combustible. Heaters are never left on all night. Extension cords can be dangerous and are never used. Heaters with oil reservoirs use an internal element to heat the oil and are safer than other types because nothing flammable is exposed. As the oil heats inside the radiator, hot air is generated and radiated throughout the room. In addition, oil heaters are energy efficient and have multiple temperature settings.

A suitably sized fire extinguisher is kept just outside the grow area along with a garden hose or other water supply. Electrical work is always done to building code standard. Electrical wiring books available in the library describe common building code requirements. Proper three-pronged grounding plugs are used for additional safety and are never cut to fit into a two-pronged outlet. Only heavy-duty timers are used. Care is taken to never overload any circuit. All elements are determined to function properly before the system is operated.

Chapter 4

Seeds

Only the best seeds are selected for hydroponic growing. Genetics plays an important role in the cultivation of plants: seeds gathered from superior marijuana plants produce superior marijuana. With ongoing gardens the seed stage can be skipped as the gardener proceeds directly to the cloning process. When cloning is not possible, the old-fashioned way is used—germinating seeds.

Germination

Seeds may be germinated in a number of different ways. A simple method is to cover several

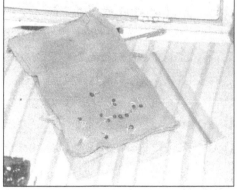

Seeds germinating on a moist washcloth.

seeds with a wet paper towel or washcloth. This is then enclosed in a small plastic bag to retain moisture and placed in a warm, dark cabinet or drawer. The towel or cloth is kept moist until the seeds germinate, which takes 3 to 10 days.

Hydroponic Germination

Hydroponic seed germination is simple. A 12 by 24 inch tray or shallow dish is used. A simple shallow dish filled about halfway full of water works well. Small three-inch hydroponic plastic cups are placed in the trays and filled with *lava rock*, a porous kernel used in various types of hydroponic gardening, to just above the water line. Seeds are placed on top of the lava rock and more lava rock is added to the cup until it is full.

Another method of germination uses two-inch rockwool cubes. In this process, the seeds are placed 1/4 inch from the top.

A third method employs small three-inch peat moss cups filled with a 50/50 combination of a coarse-grade horticultural perlite and vermiculite mixture. The peat cup is placed in the water tray and the seed is planted about 1/4 inch below the top of the non-nutrient medium.

An aquarium air pump is turned on and the bubbling wand placed in the water.

Lighting

The seeding and cloning areas are lighted with four-foot-long, single-fixture, two-tube, 40-watt grow lights. Gro™ tubes are purchased along with the fixtures.

Fluorescent lights are used for seedlings and clones.

Lights are hung two inches over the tops of the seedlings or clones, and about one foot apart. The light coverage area is six inches to either side of the tubes and, of course, the four foot length of the lights. The lights are kept turned off until the seeds germinate.

Seedlings

After germination, seedlings are transferred into small three-inch hydroponic containers and placed in the cloning or seeding trays. Seedlings are placed in the cup with their roots positioned in the water. Lava rock is poured in the cup until it reaches above the water line and

**Florescent lights hang about a foot apart
one to two inches above clones.**

just under the primary leaves of the seedling. The area is lighted after the first seeds germinate and the lights are raised as the seedlings grow so that they are always a few inches above the heads of the growing seedlings.

Each seedling quickly grows to three or four inches tall, developing a longer taproot with several lateral roots, and is then ready to be transplanted into a larger container that is placed in the pre-blooming area.

The seedlings are placed in the pre-blooming area as soon as possible to allow feeding times to be increased along with the growth rates of the plants. For this phase, a standard Ebb and Flow grow bed with a standard Ebb and Flow reservoir is used. The water is turned on and begins to cycle.

Next, the larger, plastic hydroponic containers are placed in the water. The seedling is held in the container with its roots hanging in the water while the leaves are held out of the water and lava rock is poured around the plant until it reaches just under the leaves and holds the plant in place. A 400-watt metal halide bulb is turned on.

The seedling in the photo is ready to be transplanted from the cloning tray into a larger container and moved into the pre-

Transplanting seedling.

blooming area. Different hydroponic systems require different watering schedules, which are maintained with timers.

Timers

The best timers have 30-minute on/off intervals over a 24-hour period. Timers are set to turn on the water pumps once every three or four hours to circulate the water for approximately 30 minutes and then to shut off for three or four hours.

As plants are watered daily, the time between watering is lengthened until eventually the water is circulated only once every six to eight hours for 30 minutes.

Chapter 5

Nutrients

The key to growing hydroponically is to control the nutrients that plants receive. One mistake in the amount or ratio of nutrients can wipe out a garden.

Chemical Fertilizers

Chemical fertilizers are concentrated forms of nutrients. The formulas are mixed in different ratios depending on the type of plant being fed.

Basic 3 formula General Hydroponic™ solutions (right) with pH Up™, pH Down™ and meters for pH, ppm with calibration liquids

A popular product is General Hydroponics™, which includes three formulas: *grow, bloom,* and *micro.* The grow formula has the largest concentration of nitrogen and is used for vegetative growth. The bloom formula has a higher concentration of phosphate, which is needed for blooming. The micro formula contains necessary macro-nutrients and micro-nutrients.

After the proper amount of fertilizer formula is calculated, the nutrients are thoroughly mixed with one gallon of water. Using the water as a delivery system for the nutrients disperses them more evenly throughout the water in the reservoir. This is called the "active" delivery system, because the nutrients are actively administered to the plants via the water in the reservoir as the water circulates. The nutrients are recovered in the reservoir when the watering period is over.

Organic Fertilizers

In earlier times, organic fertilizers were made from cow manure, horse manure and even fish emulsion. Today, organic fertilizers are much more refined. Mixtures derived from organic elements are combined to create clean formulas that have a full range of all the necessary primary, secondary and trace elements. Organic formulas have opened the door to organic manipulation of the growing processes. Increasingly, organic compounds and procedures are being incorporated into hydroponic growing. The Hans method is an organic method used on the mother plants or *mammas,* and on plants

during the last two weeks of blooming.

Feeding is the primary factor in producing a superior crop. Mixing nutrient

Organic nutrients for feeding mammas and wick method blooming plants.

formulas is part of the art of growing marijuana hydroponically. It requires an extensive knowledge of standard nutrients and a constant awareness of the new nutrients that are continually finding their way to the marketplace.

Primary Nutrients

The three primary nutrients are nitrogen (N), phosphorus (P) and potassium (K). Nutrients are usually listed on fertilizer labels, where the letters N, K and P will be followed by a number that designates the proportion of each respective ingredient. "N-2, K-6, P-1" means the nutrients are proportionally two percent nitrogen, six percent potassium or potash, and one percent phosphorus.

Nitrogen (N)

Nitrogen is essential for nourishing the building blocks of plants. It is the main nutrient fueling rapid growth during the vegetative state and is essential in the production of a healthy marijuana crop.

Young plant in non-nutritive medium thrives on proper amounts of nitrogen.

Nitrogen also aids the root system to penetrate the medium in order to anchor and strengthen the plant, and it helps to produce a secure structure where the leaves, stems and the physical body of the plant can flourish.

Nitrogen must be constantly replenished in proper proportions. The art of growing marijuana hydroponically lies in meeting the nitrogen needs at various stages of growth. After nitrogen has been metabolized by the plant, it is used to make chlorophyll.

Phosphorus (P)

Phosphorus facilitates every stage of a plant's life. It is employed in photosynthesis as well as in seeding and blooming, and is given to clones because it assists in the development of the root system.

Phosphorus aids the reproduction process and is a vital component of other metabolic processes.

Potassium (K)

Potassium helps in the manufacture of the sugars and starches needed for metabolism and is administered during all stages of the plant's growth. Potassium helps create strong cellular growth in the roots, stems and leaves of the plants. It is also a factor in enabling plants to resist disease.

Secondary Nutrients

The secondary nutrients Calcium (Ca), Magnesium (Mg) and Sulfur (S) are supplied in hydroponic formulas in the proper percentages. Caution is always exercised when mixing nutrient formulas. Special attention must be directed toward the different stages of growth, because they require different amounts of various nutrients.

Calcium

Calcium is used when chromosomes of cells replicate themselves just prior to cellular division. A bit of calcium is found in the tip of each root—an indication of its importance in cell growth.

Magnesium

Magnesium is the central atom in chlorophyll molecules. It facilitates use of nutrients as well as light. It is a critical factor in the plant's overall health and vigor.

Sulfur

Sulfur is found in the nitrogenous organic compounds essential to plant protein production. Sulfur helps plants use nutrients and create plant vitamins. Hydroponic nutrient solutions contain certain amounts of sulfur. Sulfur content is increased by adding Epsom salts or magnesium sulfate.

Trace Elements

The hydroponic formulas contain only minute quantities of micro, because only small amounts of these nutrients are needed to precipitate various plant processes. Supplemental trace elements are never added more than once every two weeks because too many trace elements render the water toxic which damages the plants and may kill them.

If the water reservoir accidentally receives too many trace elements, it is changed immediately. The medium is flushed at the same time by flooding the upper grow bed a couple of times with clean, non-nutritive water. The water pump timer is set to flood the upper bed once every 30 minutes. This cleansing process is repeated several times.

Trace Element Supplements

Most standard hydroponics formulas have a trace element solution. Supplemental trace elements can be added directly to the water reservoir or are foliar fed-sprayed directly on the leaves.

When additional supplements are added to the regime, about one-half of the recommended amount is added at first to determine the impact of the extra nutrients on the plants before more are added. New trace element supplements are being released on the market practically every day.

Catalysts

Catalysts are nutrients that help plants use nutrient formulas. Catalysts used as supplements are almost always trace elements. The addition of separate catalysts, other than the standard hydroponics trace elements or micro solution, are used with caution.

B1

B1 is a useful aid in preventing transplant shock, as well as stimulating root growth. It is good for starting seedlings as well as for helping clones develop roots when placed in their water. The main ingredient is thiamin hydrochloride (Vitamin B1), which is also found in the rooting solutions Ortho Up-Start™, Superthrive™ and Hormex™. These solutions can be added to the water reservoirs in small doses at the beginning of each water change.

Other supplments, such as Essential Spray™, are used as a foliate food that is applied as a spray, directly onto the leaves of the plant.

Cloning Solution

Cloning solutions come in a variety of forms: liquids, powders and gels. Liquids are generally used with clones because they can go directly into the hydroponic water system without being washed off

Clone stem is wetted and dipped in the powdered rooting medium, then placed in cloning tray of water.

the stem. Dip-N-Gro™ is a liquid that penetrates the stems of the clones immediately. A clone is placed in the solution as soon as it is cut from the mother plant; it is left for up to 30 seconds and then immediately placed in the cloning tray.

Seedling and Cloning Nutrients

The 12 by 24 inch seedling/cloning trays hold about one gallon of water when half-full. The pH of the water is measured before the nutrients are added to the water.

The manufacturer's instructions suggest a 1/2 teaspoon of each of the three formulas, which adds up to 1 1/2 teaspoons of nutrients. However as a rule of thumb when using nutrients, small amounts are added and adjusted, as needed, to larger amounts. After nutrients have been added, they cannot be removed—except by a complete change of water. Generally, it is safe to start with 1/4 to 1/8 of the suggested amount of each of the three formulas, and then a ppm reading is taken.

A 300 ppm reading in the seedling and/or cloning water reservoirs is desirable. A ppm reading of 150 after adding nutrients means the nutrient level has reached the halfway point. In this example, the same amount of nutrients would be added to the water (creating the other half of the necessary ppm) and another ppm reading is taken. If needed, a few more nutrients are added, in their proper proportions, until the desired 300 ppm reading is achieved. A pH reading is taken and adjustments made as necessary. If the pH of a small unit such as a seedling/cloning tray needs to be adjusted, only a few drops of either pH Up™ or pH Down™ is used. After a few drops are added and stirred in and a few minutes have passed, a pH reading is taken again.

Regulating the ppm and the pH of the seedling/cloning trays is an art that takes practice. It takes a certain "feel" to know how many drops of each does what. Water is added to the trays every day and changed once every week. The pH is tested and corrected at lights-on time and again before the lights are turned off. The ppm is also tested at the same time and corrected as necessary.

Pre-Blooming Nutrients

The same technique of graduated feeding is used when nutrients are added to the

Mother plant with lush foliage on 1200 ppm diet. If fed more her leaves would burn.

pre-blooming area. A small portion of the manufacturer's suggested amount of nutrient formula is added to the circulating water in the reservoir and then a ppm reading is taken. Small amounts of nutrients are added to the water reservoir until the ppm is at its desired level—between 900 and 1,200. Some experienced gardeners raise nutrient ppm to 1,900.

Seedlings remain in the pre-blooming grow beds until they reach a height of 12 to 14 inches when their gender can be determined.

Chapter 6

Healthy Water

 All water is not the same. The chlorine content of tap water in some cities is very high, for example. Allowing water to sit out for 24 hours in a wide-mouthed container such as a large bucket or plastic garbage container releases the chlorine in it, since chlorine slowly evaporates when water sits. When a water softening system is installed, water for hydroponics can be obtained by splicing into the line before it enters the water softener. In certain geographical locations, the water may be too alkaline or too acidic, both of which affect the pH of water and impact the growing process.

pH

The acidity and alkalinity levels of water are referred to as its pH. The pH is calculated on a scale of 1 to 14, with 1 being the most acidic level on the scale, 7 being neutral, and 14 being the alkaline extremity.

Maintaining a proper pH level is essential to successful hydroponic gardening. For food to be properly assimilated and metabolized, the pH of the water must be correct. If the water is not pH balanced, plants do not absorb all the nutrients suspended in it. When the pH is balanced, plants can more readily break down nutrients into usable forms.

A pH of 6.3 is considered ideal for marijuana cultivation. Keeping the pH in the water reservoir maintained at a constant 6.3 would be a daunting task. Fortunately, maintaining the pH between 5.5 and 6.9 is adequate.

Testing pH

The pH is tested in a variety of ways. Litmus paper is too crude for testing pH and is never  used. A top-of-the line pH tester is worthwhile, because of the value of accurate testing. These immediately display a digital readout of the exact pH of the water.

The pH meter is a plant's friend.

The water level and pH of the water is tested when the lights-on period begins, before any nutrients are added. The pH is tested a second time about 15 to 30 minutes after nutrients have been added and thoroughly mixed in the reservoir. If needed, the pH of the water in the reservoir is adjusted by adding chemicals designed to raise or lower the pH. These chemicals (referred to as pH Up™ and pH Down™) are available at the same outlets where pH meters are sold. I necessary, pH is adjusted again just before the lights-out period.

The cloning reservoir is small and easily contaminatedy.

A pH *buffer* solution, which is used to calibrate the pH meter to the proper setting before the pH is tested, is needed. It takes practice to be able to accurately read the meters and to use pH Up™ and pH Down™ to fine-tune the pH.

Nutrient pH

Maintaining the proper nutrient and pH balance is the most difficult aspect of hydroponic gardening. As a safety precaution, the water in the reservoir is changed once a week whether the water looks like it needs changing or not, because weekly water changes help to assure a correct nutrient (ppm) level and proper pH.

There are a number of factors that influence the ever-changing pH level of the water. Each nutrient suspended in the water reservoir has a different pH. Nutrients are consumed by the plants at different rates depending on various factors. For example, the cloning tray consumes less nutrients than a half-full blooming area does. As different nutrients are used by the plants, the pH of the water changes.

Such changes are a daily occurrence. The pH and the nutrient ppm are checked and regulated at least twice a day, at the beginning of the lights-on period and just before the lights-out period.

With experience , the ratio between the nutrient usage and the parallel change of the pH levels becomes more noticeable. As such sensitivity grows it is easier to make minute changes and maintain precise control over the pH and the ppm of the reservoirs.

Parts per Million (ppm)

After nutrients are added to the water reservoir and the pH is balanced, the plants begin to consume the food. Logically, the larger the number of plants, the more nutrients the reservoir needs. The amount of nutrients applied to the water is measured with a mechanical device called a *parts per million (ppm) meter*, which is an essential tool for hydroponic growing. The meters use a ppm calibration solution and are available at the same outlets where pH meters are sold.

The directions on the hydroponic nutrient containers indicate the proper amount of nutrient to add to the water reservoir. At first only about one-fourth of the suggested amount of nutrient solution should be added to the water reservoir. Then a ppm reading is taken, after which another quarter of the nutrient solution is added and another ppm reading is taken. Slowly increasing the amount of solution is smarter than running the risk of over-fertilizing on the first application. A ppm of 900 to 1,200 is maintained initially. Experienced gardeners sometimes maintain an even higher range of 1,200 to 1,800 ppm.

When the water cycles from the water reservoir to the grow bed the plants eat the food and digest the nutrients. The plants do not use all of the different nutrients at the same rate, which causes an immediate change in the pH, the ppm and the relationship of nutrient concentration (RNC). The change in the RNC is more difficult to calculate than the pH and ppm. When the first nutrients are applied, the RNC of the water is properly proportioned, as indicated on the label of the nutrient containers. In other words, there are specific amounts of each nutrient in each formula, which means there is a given proportion of each nutrient in the water reservoir.

Balance of Nutrients

As the plants feed, they do not consume all of the nutrients at an equal rate. Some nutrients will hardly be used at all, while others are absorbed and used more quickly. As more nutrients are added each day to make up for the loss of those assimilated by the plants, the proper balance of nutrients changes. Nutrients that are not absorbed by the plants build up, causing an imbalance in the proper RNC. When this happens, the water becomes toxic and unusable, even though the ppm meter reading indicates that there is a proper amount of nutrient in the water and everything appears to be fine.

This happens because the ppm meter indicates only how many parts per million there are of nutrients in the water. The meter does not indicate if the nutrients are at balanced or toxic levels. This is the reason that the water is changed at least once a week. Changing the water maintains the proper RNC. If the nutrient solution has been compromised in any way, the water in the reservoir is changed and nutrients are not added for at least a day while the plants are observed to see if any damage has occurred. As a precaution, the medium is leached (drained slowly) with pure water a few times.

Signs of Over-feeding

Over-feeding initially creates the appearance that the plants are doing great, because they look lush and green, and show rapid growth. Growth that is faster than normal is suspicious and should be closely monitored. When the tips of the lush, green leaves turn yellow, reddish-yellow or even blackish-green, there is a problem. In the case of severe burn, the tips and edges of the plant's leaves curl under. The more severe the burn, the more pronounced the deep coloring and the curl-under.

Too Much Fertilizer

Too much fertilizer can kill the plants. If the hydroponic garden has been over-fertilized, the water in the reservoir is changed and feeding is stopped until all indications of over-feeding have subsided. Flushing the medium helps. The main indication that the plant has absorbed all excess nutrients is a lighter coloring and no signs of burn on the new growth: this usually takes only a few days to occur.

Oxygenating the Reservoir

Additional oxygen is added to water and applied to the plants at various stages. This is especially true of the Ebb and Flow method . Additional oxygen in the water means more oxygen is available to

Aquarium air pump oxygenates the water.

the roots of the plants. Oxygen in the water assists nutrients to flow more efficiently into the root structure.

Aquarium pumps work best for oxygenating the reservoir. To

determine the size of the air pump needed, the gallon capacity is added to the three (or more) places that will be aerated. If a pump supplies enough oxygen for a 50 gallon fish tank, then 50 gallons of reservoir is properly supplied and serviced by the same size pump.

Oxygenating Water

Oxygenating the water can be easily done with a three-way splitter, to which pre-measured lengths of hose and three or more bubbling wands are attached. Three-way air splitters receive air in one inlet and allow air out the three separate outlets. Each outlet has its own screw-type control that allows only a certain amount of air to exit the hose, thus permitting different amounts of air to be sent to different hoses and reservoirs.

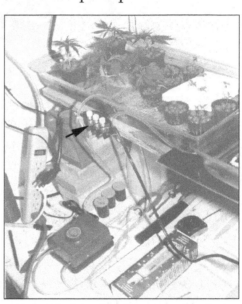

Aquarium pump has three-outlet control. One hose goes to clones, one to pre-blooming reservoir, and one to blooming reservoir.

Controls on the three-way splitter can be manipulated so that the small reservoir receives less

air while the larger reservoirs receive proportionately larger shares. The hose connects to the aquarium

Bubbling wand oxygenates the water.

pump and air outlet, which is attached into the three-way splitter. Air is sent into the water of the cloning reservoir via a hose with a small (about four-inch) bubbling wand.

A second hose with a larger wand directs air into the larger pre-blooming reservoir. The third air hose is directed into the blooming area, which is the largest of all the areas and uses the largest bubbling wand.

Different grow areas require different reservoir flooding schedules. For an initial setting, timers are set to cycle the water every four hours. The time between each watering is then lengthened by a half hour, until one or more plants indicate a need for water. For example, if it takes eight hours before the first plant needs water, then the watering cycle can be safely set to water every six hours.

Chapter 7

Ebb and Flow Method

The Ebb and Flow (E&F) setup requires a lower water reservoir and an upper grow bed. The water rests in the reservoir until it is needed in the grow bed, where it is periodically pumped by an aquarium water pump with backflow ability. The pump has a clear plastic hose placed flush with the bottom of the grow bed and is glued into place with aquarium sealant.

The timer starts the pump and circulates the water once every four to six hours. Water enters the inlet and rises to the level of the overflow tubes before it is returned to the reservoir. The water circulates until the timer on the water pump shuts off; then it flows back down the same hose.

The E&F grow bed is fashioned to hold the plants plus a standing level of five to six inches of water. In addition, there is enough water in the reservoir to keep the pump completely submerged as water circulates from the top of the grow bed to the reservoir. When circulation stops, the water in the system flows back

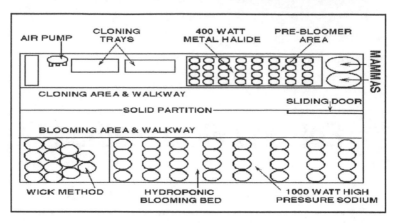

**Top view of E & F setup,
showing cloning and blooming areas.**

down into the reservoir. The water level in
the reservoir when all the water has flowed
back into it is the minimum amount of water
needed for the system to work properly. A few
more inches of water is added to the reservoir
to compensate for water use and evaporation.
Water is also added daily to keep the level
above the minimum required.

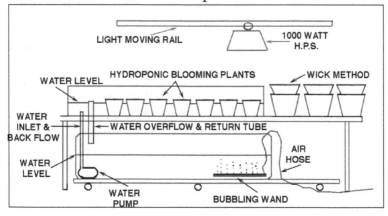

Side view of E &F blooming area.

The E&F Cycle

Ten plants are transferred into the blooming area every two weeks. Water flows upward from the water pump into the reservoir, reaches the top of the overflow tube and returns to the reservoir. The water circulates for 30 minutes before the pump is automatically shut off by a timer. Then water flows back down the inlet tube through the water pump as it completely empties the upper grow bed. Also, on a two-week cycle, the 10 plants with the most buds are placed into a wick method setup.

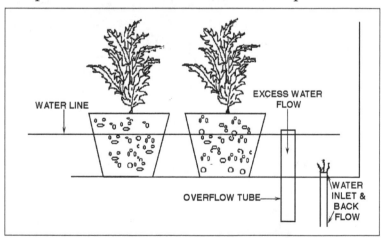

E&F water circulation system.

Growing Mediums

Because the E&F method and Nutrient Film/Flow Technique (NFT), which will be covered next, are both medium friendly, a variety of growing media can be used during all stages of growth—from clones to pre-bloomers to blooming plants. Most hydroponic growers prefer either the lava rock or rockwool as media or strata. Inert media, such as coconut fiber or perlite/vermiculite mixtures, work well with both of these methods.

Lava Rock

Lava rock is available in any number of small pea-to-marble-sized porous hydroponic grow media. These versatile nuggets can hold water for long

Clones in lava rock.

periods of time and assist the capillary action of water. They are used for seedlings, clones and pre-blooming and blooming plants.

Clone in rockwool.

Rockwool

Rockwool may also be used at all stages of the growing process. Small two-inch cubes are perfect for clones and are placed on larger rockwool units for pre-blooming and blooming. They are suitable for both the E&F and the NFT processes.

B Perlite/Vermiculite Mixture

A combination of perlite and vermiculite is easy to obtain and makes an excellent inert strata. This mixture is excellent for clones and can be placed in a number of different containers. Mixed medium can be placed in the bottom half of a milk jug

Clones in perlite/vermiculite.

with holes punched in the bottom and sides, for example. This could be placed in the grow beds and function as well as any other medium for any stage of growth. It is widely available and is not expensive, especially when purchased in four-cubic-foot units.

Other Media

There are many other media, including coconut fiber and rubber-type foam, that work well in hydroponic gardens. Ease, safety and availability are considered to determine the best medium to use.

Chapter 8

Film/Flow Technique

The setup and structure for the Nutrient Film/Flow Technique (NFT) are different than those for the E&F method. The key words in this process are *film* and *flow*. A structure allows a thin flow or film to wash over the roots. The most common device used for NFT grow beds is a standard plastic pipe or standard rain gutter.

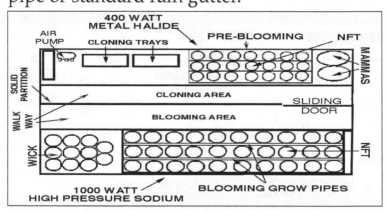

**Top view of cloning and blooming areas
of Nutrient Film/Flow setup**

In the NFT setup structure, grow beds in the pre-blooming and blooming areas are constructed of plastic pipes. The pipes have end covers, allowing them to be used as containers. Pipes are used as the top growing bed, running parallel to each other. As many pipes as are needed to fill the space allocated are used. The pipes are spaced 8 to 12 inches apart, depending on how big the plants are expected to grow: the smaller the plants, the closer the spacing. Holes are cut 8 to 12 inches apart in the tops of the pipes, again depending on the size of the plants placed in them.

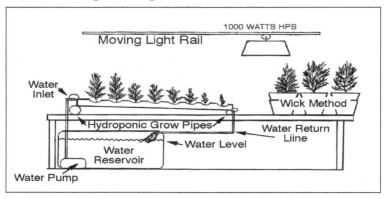

Nutrient Flim/Flow Technique blooming area.

The holes are cut to the same size as the containers that fit into them, and the pipes sit at a slight angle to facilitate the flow of water delivered to the raised end of each pipe. The end where the water enters is raised about 1 inch, so that the water exits the opposite end. There are a number of configurations used for the reservoir and grow bed combination. Most commonly the reservoir is placed at the lower end of the grow pipes.

The Reservoir

Reservoirs are made from expensive manufactured water reservoirs, plain plastic tubs or even simple plastic trays. Sometimes reservoirs are handmade from wooden frames lined with plastic or painted with the water-resistant paint used for swimming pools.

The purpose of the reservoir is to hold the water as it is recycled through the upper grow bed pipes with a small aquarium pump. A single hose carries the water to a delivery pipe that dispenses the water evenly into each separate pipe, after which the water is sent to each pipe via a small hose or tube.

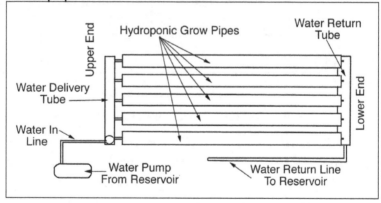

Top view of NFT water delivery and return system.

The water is gravity-fed from the delivery pipe, which sits atop the grow pipes. After the water flows down to the lower end of the grow pipes, it is collected in the return tube and returned by gravity to the reservoir. Sometimes a single large hose is used, which splits off into as many separate hoses as there are pipes, each pipe getting its own hose.

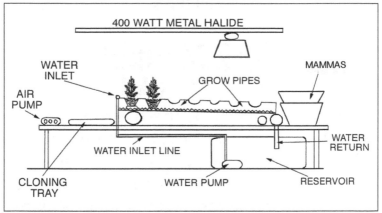

Pre-blooming area of Nutrient Flim/Flow Technique

Nutrient water is pumped up the hose into the raised end of the pipes, so that it can run down the pipes into contact with the bottom of the plant containers, where it wets the containers, the plant roots and whatever medium is used.

The flow of water need only be 1/4 to 1/2 an inch deep to maintain a correct moisture content in the roots of the plants. The water flows through the pipes and feeds the plants. When the water arrives at the lower end of the grow bed pipes, it is returned to the reservoir.

Sometimes a single length of pipe catches all the water as it drains from the pipes. Sometimes each pipe has its own return hose. Water runs continuously and is changed once a week.

Chapter 9

Wick Method

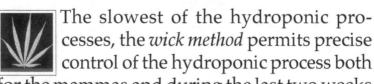The slowest of the hydroponic processes, the *wick method* permits precise control of the hydroponic process both for the mammas and during the last two weeks of the blooming period. A single plant is placed in a grow bed container and another container is used as a reservoir. The grow bed container has nylon wicks similar to those used in kerosene lamps coming out the bottom to deliver water and nutrients to the upper plant, which never comes into contact with the water in the lower, single-container reservoir.

Wick Method for Mammas

Female mother plants can be kept in the same hydroponic grow bed as the pre-bloomers, or in a separate hydroponic grow bed and reservoir in the cloning area. The drawback to these two techniques is that the mammas will have the same feeding schedule as the pre-bloomers if they are kept in the same grow bed. On the other hand, creating a separate hydroponic grow bed and reservoir involves an additional pump and other duplicate equipment. This can generate a lot of unnecessary work and may not be as effective as the wick method.

Mother plants need a different feeding schedule than pre-bloomers. Pre-bloomers are fed a constant high-nitrogen, fast-lane nutrient diet. The mother plants are placed on a high-nitrogen feeding schedule after cloning for only one week. During the following week, the mother plants are fed a low-nitrogen diet. This will create a low-nitrogen, high-carbohydrate mother plant that will produce faster-rooting clones. The wick method facilitates an altered feeding schedule while addressing other major concerns.

Items needed to create a simple wick method environment for mammas

• A large container, such as a 10-inch standard plastic plant container with pre-cut holes in the bottom, to be used as a grow bed.

• Four to eight single, one-inch-wide, nylon wick-like pieces of strapping for use as wicks, each cut to an appropriate length.

• A second 10-inch plastic container with no holes in the bottom, to serve as a water reservoir.

• A medium, consisting of equal parts lava rock, horticultural perlite and vermiculite.

• A small plastic cup to sit in the bottom of the reservoir as a support for the grow bed.

With the wick method, it does not matter which medium clones are rooted in. Whether rockwool, lava rock or perlite/vermiculite is used, the process is still the same.

First, a grow bed for the new mamma is created. Wicks of appropriate length are placed in the grow containers. The wicks are placed inside the containers starting at the top inner edge, travel down the sides and exit the bottom through the pre-cut drain holes. The wicks extend about six to eight inches from the bottom of the grow container, which can be as large as desired.

The female plant, which resides in the smaller six-to-eight-inch container it was rooted in, is placed in the 10-inch grow container until the tops of the two containers are even. A mark is placed where the bottom of the smaller container reaches to about the middle of the larger container. Then the lava rock/perlite/vermiculite mixture is poured into the grow container until it rises to the mark made by the bottom of the smaller container. The plant is taken out of the smaller container and placed on top of this mixture, so the top of the smaller transplants medium and the top of the larger container are even.

Containers for wick method. Wicks extend from bottom of grow medium container. Nested wick-method containers.

The remainder of the 10-inch container is filled the rest of the way around the sides of the smaller container within it. The non-nutrient mixture holds the wicks, which are tucked just under the top of the mixture, in place.

The combination of media and the capillary action of the wicks allows more precise control of the watering and nutrient uptake of the mother plants. After the grow bed has been created, it is placed into the lower water reservoir.

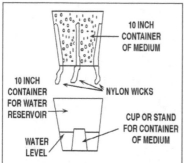

A small cup sits upside down in the bottom on the container which is used as a water reservoir.

A small cup sits upside down in the bottom of the water reservoir. These units only need to be watered every few days, and the reservoir is drained completely before any more water is added. It is not filled on a daily basis unless, of course, all the water is used daily.

A small four-to-six-inch plastic container is placed in the bottom center of the 10-inch plas-tic reservoir container. If a six-inch-high container is used, then the 10-inch plastic container is filled with only five inches of water. This assures that when the 10-inch plastic container being used as the grow bed is placed in the 10-inch reservoir, the

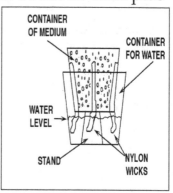

Only the wicks sit in the water.

bottom of the grow bed container will not be touching the water. It will, instead, remain one inch above the water line. Filling the reservoir with water only and never placing nutrients in it insures that the mother plants are fed nothing but totally organic nutrients. About once every three days a weak solution of organic nutrients is delivered to the mother plant through the top of the grow container.

The nutrients are mixed with one cup of water, which is administered onto the top of the medium in the grow container. The reservoir is allowed to dry almost completely about every three days to allow the roots to breathe. The dry medium is slightly watered before fertilizing; mammas are never fertilized when the medium is dry. A weak solution of organic nutrients is mixed with one cup of water and poured over the pre-moistened medium.

If a little nutrient water drains into the reservoir it is simply removed. A few hours later, the water reservoir is filled only to the point where it will become totally dry again in three days.

If an organic formula nutrient calls for a teaspoon of nutrient in a gallon of water once a week, then the mother is given only 1/8 teaspoon in one cup of water. The process is repeated two to three days later. The plant's needs are observed and regulated to determine if the amount given was adequate for the plant during the three-day period. Less nutrients are given at first and more is added only when necessary. Light green-colored leaves indicate a need for more food. When the leaves display a rich, dark-green color, the proper amount of food for the mamma has been found.

Using Wick at End of Blooming

The wick method is used during the last two weeks of blooming to control water usage and nutrient uptake, and washes out the chemicals used when feeding in the standard hydroponic grow bed during the initial part of the plants' blooming time.

Blooming plants may be fully bloomed in the standard blooming area. They will, however, retain chemical residue from the standard feeding which is applied to the reservoir. A separate, nutrient free hydroponic area may be created for them if the wick method is not used.

Chapter 10

Cloning

After the seedlings have been in the pre-blooming area for two weeks, they should have reached a height of 12 to 14 inches and will be ready to have their gender determined. The process is quite simple. The cloning area is prepared and a clone is taken from each plant.

The clone and plant it came from are identically marked for identification. The fluorescent light that was used for the seedlings is temporarily placed in the blooming area and used for these clones. The clones only receive 12 hours of light each day under fluorescent grow lights. The parent seedlings remain in the pre-blooming area under the 400-watt metal halide bulb with an 18-hour light schedule.

Cloning

The first step in cloning is gathering all the proper tools and materials needed for the cloning area.

Nodes are the places on the plant where the main stem, leaf and lateral branches come together to form an axis. The spaces between the nodes are called internodes. There are anywhere from four to eight nodes on the parent seedlings.

Cloning Tools

- Sharp razor blade or utility knife.
- Cloning tray, 12 by 24 inch rooting tray.
- Cloning solution, such as Dip-N-Gro™.
- Plant starter, such as Ortho Up-Start™ with B1 rooting solution.
- Growing medium, such as rockwool cubes or lava rock.

Clones are ideally about four inches long. The razor blade is used to make a cut about four inches from the top of the plant. The cut is made at a 45 degree angle. Making the cut just above a node creates a clone with a small portion remaining that will act as a stem.

As soon as it is cut, the clone is placed into the cloning solution for about 10 to 30 seconds, depending on the liquid penetration desired. Next it is placed into the medium of choice. When using cloning powder, the stem of the clone is wetted prior to dipping to help the powder adhere (see photo page 31).

The growing medium is kept ready in the cloning tray, which is filled about halfway with water. Prior to planting the clones the proper amount of any rooting starter which has B1, such as Super Thrive™ or Hormex™ is

Clone is cut just above the next to lower node to create a clone with a long bottom stem.

Two heads will grow.

added to the water and the ppm is adjusted to 300. The pH is balanced at 6.3 after the ppm has been established. Horticultural heating pads placed under the cloning trays are conducive to root growth.

After Cloning

After a clone is taken from each parent seedling, the seedlings are placed back into the pre-blooming area under 400-watt metal halide lighting. Temperature levels in the reservoirs are maintained between 65° and 76°F degrees and are never allowed to exceed 80°F, which would foster organic growths that consume nutrients and upset the standard pH and ppm.

The tops of the reservoirs are covered, as light promotes the growth of destructive organisms in the water. Tepid water is used when the water in the reservoir is changed, because water temperatures below 65°F are detrimen-

tal to the growth process.

The reservoir holding the parent seedlings needs daily maintenance. The pH and ppm

Clones in simple grow reservoir.

of the reservoir are checked morning and evening and adjusted as necessary. The reservoir ppm is maintained in the 900 to 1,200 range and light is allowed to shine on the plants for 18 hours.

A metal halide light on a rail or track move over the parent seedlings creating a phototropic environment for the plants. The room temperature is kept around 76°F—always a few degrees above the temperature of the water in the reservoir, to avoid excess evaporation.

The parent seedlings sit in the pre-blooming area for approximately two weeks while they increase in size. After a week has passed, the two topmost growing terminals are pinched to create a four-headed plant. The water in the reservoir continues to be changed at least once every week.

The clones in the cloning trays sit in the blooming area and are tended every day on the same schedule as the parent seedlings. The pH and ppm is checked twice a day and adjustments are made. The ppm of the cloning tray is kept at 300, the fluorescent grow lights are left on for 12 hours a day and the water in the tray is changed weekly. If there is difficulty maintaining the proper pH or ppm, the water is changed at least once every three days. Spray-misting the plants a few times a day with tepid, sodium-free distilled water invigorates the clones.

The parent seedlings and the clones continue to grow for about two weeks in their respective environments. After about two weeks, the clones will have grown a few inches and developed some foliage and tiny root systems. Most important, the tips and nodes of the clones will begin to show gender.

Chapter 11

Gender Identification

Identifying gender is very important because it is the female plants that produce the highly prised smoking buds. Males must be identified and discarded. To accomplish this, gardeners must be able to tell the two sexes apart.

Females

On some plants, small bud-shaped growths that can be seen with a magnifying glass appear at the nodes and tip of the growing terminal. At first, all the buds look the same, but upon closer inspection, different characteristics are detected.

Female bud or bract appearing in axis of node

Some of the small buds have a more elongated shape than the others. These more elongated buds have two tiny white or yellowish hairs protruding from them. *Bracts*, as they are called, form in small clusters, with the hairs soon becoming the most prominent visual feature. These characteristics indicate that the plant is a female, and their presence in a clone is an indication that the parent seedling is also female. In growing marijuana, it is the female plant that is most highly prized.

Bract.

Males

Under a magnifying glass, some of the clones exhibit growths that do not have the more pronounced elongated shape or tiny little hairs, instead about half the bud-shaped

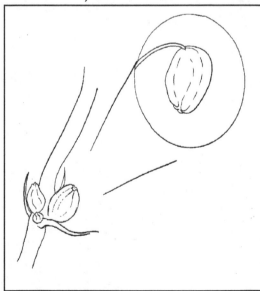

growths are more bulbous and cluster in tight groups like grapes growing from small stalks and look like small nuts. These characterize male plants.

Male bud is a rounded nut shape.

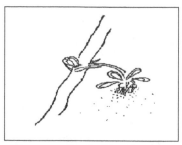

Stamens look like flowers when releasing pollen.

When a clone has been sexed as male, it is discarded along with the parent seedling from which it came. Male buds can often confuse growers, because male stamens open and display characteristics similar to a flower when releasing pollen.

Hermaphrodites

It is difficult to determine the gender of some clones or plants, because traits of both sexes are displayed. Males are removed from the growing area because they can prematurely pollinate blooming crops to prevent production of sinsemilla buds.

Male (left) and female (right).

Mammas

After the gender of all the plants has been determined, production of a never-ending supply of clones, pre-bloomers and buds begins. The cloning tray set up for determining gender is dismantled. The lighting, trays, heating pads and other materials are returned to the cloning area for future use.

The very best mammas are chosen for future cloning. As a rule of thumb, for every 15 clones desired, a mamma is kept. All other parent seedling female plants are either discarded or placed in the blooming area (novice gardeners can gain experience with hydroponic blooming areas using expendable plants). In the meantime, the cloning process begins on a regularly scheduled basis with the mammas.

A young mamma.

When mammas are selected to produce the total number of clones desired, the cloning process begins its two-week schedule. In a typical garden, the production of two mamma plants fills a full 12 by 24 inch cloning tray with clones every two weeks. This amounts to at least 15 clones from each plant, for a total of 30 clones. Every two weeks, the best 15 clones are chosen for pre-blooming, while the best eight to 10 of the pre-bloomers are placed into bloom, eventually producing eight to 10 mega-buds every two weeks.

A young mamma like the one pictured on the previous page will produce many clones in the next six months. After that, she will be replaced with a fresh mamma.

Chapter 12

Blooming and Harvesting

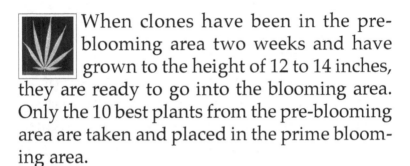When clones have been in the pre-blooming area two weeks and have grown to the height of 12 to 14 inches, they are ready to go into the blooming area. Only the 10 best plants from the pre-blooming area are taken and placed in the prime blooming area.

Blooming

Marijuana plants are photoperiodic, which means that they will continue to grow in the vegetative state as long as they receive 18 hours of light per day. However, once the light period is lowered to 12 hours per day, the plant switches to the blooming or flowering state. After two weeks on the 12 hours per day light cycle, clones will show signs of the blooming state.

Two weeks after the first set of clones has been transferred, a second set of 10 plants is placed in the blooming area. At this point, the blooming area will be half-filled with 20 plants, 10 of which will be nearing bloom.

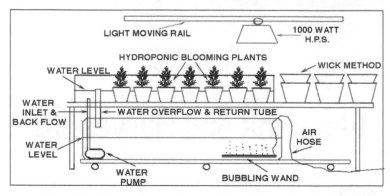

LIGHT MOVING RAIL

1000 WATT
H.P.S.

HYDROPONIC BLOOMING PLANTS

WATER LEVEL

WICK METHOD

WATER
INLET &
BACK FLOW

WATER OVERFLOW & RETURN TUBE

AIR
HOSE

WATER
LEVEL

WATER
PUMP

BUBBLING WAND

**When the first 10 plants about to bloom a second 10
plants are placed into blooming area.**

After another two weeks, a third set of 10 plants is transferred. At this point, the first set of plants should have buds that are quite bulbous, and a number of their tiny white pistils will have turned red. These plants develop a

Starting to bloom.

tremendous quantity of resin glands and have a strong sweet smell. These tiny, ball-tipped stalked glands are translucent at first. Some of the plants may have been glossed over and will have turned opaque. This is a sign that the plant is close to being ready for harvest.

Exposing the plant to the wick method (see Chapter 9) during the last two weeks before harvest allows the blooming plant to receive feeding water and small amounts of organic nutrients. The final week before harvest, the plant is given water only and no nutrients. Some gardeners give the plant only water and no food at all during the last 10 days. This forces the plant to use only the chemical nutrients already found in it. This usage of most of the relative nutrients in the plant before harvest creates a cleaner, better tasting, more desirable sweet mega-bud.

Harvesting

The schedule of the harvest is determined by carefully monitoring the plants. Once every two to three weeks is the most common time to schedule a harvest.

One grower with a small growing room harvested every week. Her cloning area was 3 by 3

Bud ready to harvest.

feet while her blooming area was 8 by 4 feet. The blooming area accommodated a maximum of 40 plants at any given time.

She had two mother plants, from which five clones were taken once a week. After three weeks, she had 30 clones. It took

three weeks for the clones to develop nice roots. After the clones rooted, she transplanted the best five into larger six-inch hydroponic containers and placed them in the pre-blooming grow bed.

After three more weeks, the clones in the pre-blooming

Pinching the top of this plant created a two-headed mega-bud.

grow bed grew to the height of 12 to 14 inches and were ready to flower. Since she cloned and transplanted every week, she could place five pre-bloomers into the blooming area once a week. It was not long before the five plants, which only needed eight weeks to totally bloom, were being harvested once a week.

Another Approach

Another grower's plants needed eight weeks to totally bloom, but his plants only needed two weeks to develop nice roots. He grow areas were exactly the same size as the previous grower's. His schedule, however, was different: He created 10 clones from each mother plant every two weeks. He then took 10 to 15 of the best 20 clones and transplanted them into the hydroponic pre-blooming area every subsequent two weeks. Next, every two weeks he moved 10 of the best 12- to 14-inch pre-bloomers over to the hydroponic blooming area. Eventually, he was harvesting 10 mega-plants every 14 days.

Timing

The examples illustrate the two main factors in determining the number of clones needed and when to take them: the time it takes the clones to root and the time it takes a given variety of marijuana to bloom fully.

The exact timing of any individual first crop is arbitrary, taking into consideration all unknown factors, but once the initial crop has been successful and the crop is on perpetual harvest schedule all the variable elements will have been established. Only then can a particular schedule of cloning, transplanting and harvesting be accurately established.

Demonstration Model

The demonstration model used in the daily routine (see Appendix) illustrates a schedule in which a grower created clones that rooted in two weeks and bloomed fully in eight weeks. This model is based on a previous exposure to the reduced rate of 12 hours a day under a 1,000 watt high-pressure sodium (HPS) light.

Hanging buds have ventilaton to dry.

Drying

The plants are trimmed of all large leaves. Some growers trim very close, while others may leave some of the smaller leaves on the plant. The plants are then hung upside down in a cool, dark place that has some ventilation. Damp conditions during drying can cause grey mold to grow. A fan helps eliminate dampness and humidity in the drying area.

After a one-to-three-week period the plants will be dry and ready for sampling. Marijuana dried for a two-to-three-week period is preferred, because plants produce more psychoactive substances when they are dried longer.

The trimmings are often saved for making marijuana butter, oil or flour for cooking.

A picture is worth a thousand words!

Appendix A

Daily Routine

 After the grow area has been built, the environmental requirements created and the mammas planted, a maintenance routine is established. This requires different actions on weekly, semiweekly and even daily cycles. After a routine is in place, the growing process becomes a smooth operation.

Day 1

The first set of clones is created when the mammas are able to produce the required quantity of clones. The clones are placed into the 12 by 24 inch cloning trays. Heating pads are turned on under the cloning trays, and the aquarium air pump is adjusted so that a moderate amount of air bubbles are produced by the bubbling wand.

A growing medium is chosen according to the grower's preference: some growers clone on Rockwool cubes, others prefer lava rock. Another possibility is floating Styrofoam™ slabs with small holes cut into them. The clone is placed through the hole with the cut bottom of the stem resting in the water of the cloning tray and the top vegetative part of the clone sitting just above the top of the Styrofoam™.

Distilled water is best for the clone reservoir, but is not required. When all the clones have been placed in the cloning tray, the condition of the water is set. First a pH reading is taken and noted. Then just enough nutrients are added to create a 300 ppm environment in the cloning reservoir. The water is stirred and a few minutes are allowed to pass before another ppm reading is taken to determine if any adjustment is needed. When the desired 300 ppm level is reached, the pH of the reservoir is taken again. Adjustments are made in the pH until the desired 6.3 level is reached.

A temperature range of 65° to 76°F degrees is maintained. The water temperature is kept a few degrees cooler than the ambient room temperature, and water is added daily as needed. The ppm and pH are also adjusted daily. The clones are examined every day to note their progress and condition. After awhile, any deviation from the clones' normal, progressive nature and growth patterns can be noticed.

When the mammas are cloned, they are not simply put under the light again. The mother plant has gone through some changes and requires extra care, including a feeding of either chemical or organic nitrogen. Some growers give their mammas a standard, organic vegetative feeding and then place about 1/2 teaspoon of organic, high-nitrogen, pasteurized worm castings on top of the medium and lightly blend it into the top inch of the medium.

For the first week after cloning, the mother plant is watered from the top of the container using two cups of water, which leaches the worm castings through the root system of the plant. After the first week, the plant is watered using the standard reservoir and weak low-nitrogen solutions are administered to the mamma.

The mother plant needs the nitrogen to stimulate vegetative growth just after cloning. A week before cloning, the nitrogen content in the feeding is reduced, which creates a clone with more carbohydrates. Growers generally prefer small feedings every three days to larger feedings every week. At this point the pre-blooming area is empty.

The mammas and clones are tended daily while waiting for the next cloning period. During this lull, growers check all the systems and observe their plants' changes. Within two weeks the clones will have grown a bit, developed more leaves and created roots that are growing out of the bottoms of the clones and their medium. Sometimes it may take three weeks for suitable root growth to appear, because of the variations in the length of time it takes the particular environment to root clones. The schedule of cloning is always set on a two-week basis.

Day 7

When the clones have been in the cloning area for seven days, it is time to change the water. Care is taken not to shock the plants with cold water. Instead, water temperature is maintained at the level to which the clones have become acclimated, usually between 65° and 75°F.

The used cloning tray is exchanged for a fresh, clean one. The air delivery wand and delivery tube are washed off with a one percent solution of common bleach and water. The water temperature gauge is also cleaned. The new water is chemically balanced, keeping the pH at 6.3 and the ppm at 300.

When the clones are growing under fluorescent lighting, the bulb is kept about one to two inches above the tops of the plants. When a 400-watt metal halide lamp is used as the light source, the tops of the clones are at least three feet from the bottom of it. When the metal halide lighting source is moving on a rail, it should be kept at least two feet from the clones. When the clones become accustomed to the powerful metal halide lighting, the plants may be slowly moved closer to the light. It takes about a week or so for the clones to adapt. After about week, the plants are moved a few inches each day until their tops are at the proper distance from the bottom of the light bulb.

A mother plant growing in the wick system is placed on the standard, general purpose, low-nitrogen feeding schedule. The plant is watered by using the lower-tier water reservoir. Feeding, too,may be accomplished in this manner when using man-made chemicals. Organic nutrients can be mixed with a cup or so of water and poured directly over the medium of choice.

When it is stationary, the top of the metal halide should be at least 12 to 24 inches from the top of the mother plant. When the light is moving on a rail or track, it may be as close as one foot from the tops of the mother plants.

A properly pruned plant looks like a flat-topped hedge with the various tops all approximately the same distance from the light source. The lights are set further away from a plant in the beginning, moving it a little closer every few days.

Day 14

After 14 days, most of the clones will have developed small root systems. At this point, the fresh water is released to the pre-blooming reservoir and started circulating into the pre-blooming grow bed. Next, the pH is checked to make sure it is at the 6.3 level. The first set of rooted clones are transplanted into the larger six-inch hydroponic containers using only lava rock as a medium.

The water in the pre-blooming grow reservoir is set to maintain a five-inch water level in the grow bed and set to cycle every five hours for a period of 30 minutes. The second controller on the aquarium air pump is adjusted as air is released into the bubbling wand, which is placed at the bottom of the pre-blooming water reservoir.

A smaller than recommended amount of nutrient is added using the three-part formula of hydroponic food. The ppm is tested and corrected. Once the desired ppm is attained, the final pH is taken and a final adjustment made, if necessary. After the clones are transported to the pre-blooming area, the cloning area sits empty. Each time the clones are transplanted, more clones are required to replace them.

The next 15 clones are taken from each mother plant, which yields a total of 30 clones. The clones are placed in fresh, clean trays and the chemical ppm and pH are adjusted.

The mother plants begin their high-nitrogen diet as they attempt to grow fresh, new clones for the next two weeks. Given a high-nitrogen diet for the first week, the plants create lush new vegetative growth. The feeding is administered in small doses every three days or so.

The clones, pre-bloomers and mother plants are monitored as the week goes on. Daily calculations are determined in each reservoir and all environmental requirements are kept within their proper parameters. Each plant is examined every day and all changes are noted; observation is the key to success with all beginning crops.

Day 21

Tasks on the 21st day are not as detailed as the previous week. Every second week is usually busier in hydroponic growing. On the 21st day, the clone bed water is changed even if it seems adequate. New trays are filled with fresh water and the thermometer and bubbler items are also cleaned. The chemical pH and ppm are properly maintained.

The same routine is undertaken in the pre-blooming bed. The water is changed and the reservoir and grow bed are cleaned, as are the thermometer, bubbling wand and air hose. Fresh water is placed in the reservoir and circulated. The chemical balance of pH 6.3 and ppm of 900 to 1,200 is achieved.

The mother plants are started on the low-nitrogen diet to allow a buildup of needed carbohydrates in the stems of the plants that will soon become new clones. A spray misting of tepid water twice daily assists in leaching the nitrogen out of the leaves of the plants. They are watered using the lower water reservoir and fed by pouring a cup of nutrient water on top of the medium of the upper grow container.

Cleaning continuously is standard maintenance. The underside of the leaves are checked for pests and all systems are checked to make sure everything is in proper order.

Day 28

The first clones, which were placed in the pre-blooming area two weeks earlier, will have grown to the height of 12 to 14 inches and be ready to go into the blooming area. The blooming area lights must be turned on. All environmental requirements located in or associated with the blooming area are prepared and the water reservoir is filled and all elements are turned on. Only the 10 best plants from the pre-blooming area are taken and placed in the prime blooming area. After the pre-bloomers are taken from the cloning area and placed into the blooming area, the nutrient ppm and pH of the water are properly set. The ppm of the water in the blooming area is set to the same level as the ppm of the water in the pre-blooming area: from 900 to 1,200.

The difference in the nutrient solution is very important. In the blooming area the plants are given the Flora Bloom™ formula. It is no longer necessary for the nutrient feeding formulations to conform to the vegetative requirements of the plant. The plants in the blooming area require the blooming nutrient formula. The vegetative formula is always used in the cloning area and the blooming formula in the blooming area.

After the pre-bloomers are moved over to the blooming area, the clones, which have developed roots, are ready to be transported to the pre-blooming area. The pre-blooming area is thoroughly cleaned before transplanting the new clones into it. This means that the grow bed, the reservoir and all associated materials and devices are thoroughly washed. Fresh water is placed in the water reservoir and the newly rooted clones are transplanted into the clean pre-blooming area. Again the ppm and pH are adjusted.

A new tray is filled with water and receives the new clones. After the clones are placed in the cloning tray, the pH 6.3 and ppm are corrected. The mother plant is placed back on the high-nitrogen feeding schedule. The plants are tended daily paying special attention to the ppm and the pH as well as to the plants' appearance to determine if they are over- or under-fed.

Day 35

By the 35th day, the schedule is routine, down to mostly watering- and maintenance-related. The area and items are cleaned and new water is added to the cloning reservoir while maintaining the proper pH and ppm levels.

The water in the pre-blooming reservoir is also changed and all associated parts are cleaned. The reservoir is replenished and the water is re-circulated. Once again, ppm and pH are properly adjusted.

In the blooming area, the water reservoir is changed and cleaned. The new water is chemically balanced. The blooming formula of the three-solution nutrient food is fed in the blooming area.

The mother plants are placed on low-nitrogen feeding. Any excess or crowded stems on the parent plant are pruned. The mother plant needs to retain just enough arms and branches to produce a few more clones than a grower will actually need. The mother plant is periodically pruned to a shape that is squat, rounded, flat-topped and bushy, with the non-pruned arms or branches evenly spaced.

Day 42

The second set of 10 plants is placed in the blooming area. At this point, the blooming area will be half-filled with 20 plants. Of course, before this change, the water in the blooming reservoir must be emptied. The grow bed and the reservoir are cleaned. Fresh water must be cycled in the blooming system and pH and ppm must be corrected.

The emptied pre-blooming area is also purged of the old water. The area is cleaned and new water is cycled into the system. Newly rooted clones are placed in the pre-blooming area into larger containers. Again, pH and ppm are properly adjusted. The cloning areas are cleared of plants to replace the cloning tray with a fresh tray filled with clean water. The mother plants are cloned and the cloning tray is filled with fresh-cut clones. The water in the cloning tray is prepared and the bubbling wand is turned on. The mother plant is given a little more nitrogen in her diet.

Day 49

The water in all the reservoirs is changed, cleaned and replenished with fresh nutrients. In addition, the amount of nitrogen in the mother plants' food is lowered. At this time the water in the pre-blooming and blooming reservoirs may be allowed to remain for up to one more week, so the correct water balance is maintained for two weeks instead of one.

At the start of the second week, if any of the plants show adverse effects, the water reservoir is changed immediately and the chemical pH and ppm are rebalanced. Unskilled growers change the water every week to insure that pH and ppm are correct.

As growers develop the skill of controlling ppm of the pre-blooming and blooming reservoirs at around 1,200 ppm, they usually go on to the higher 1,300 and 1,800 ppm levels. This is done by increasing the ppm by 100 points every day or so until the proper ppm is obtained. If signs of burning or over-fertilizing appear, the application of nutrients is immediately stopped until the symptoms disappear. In case of severe burn, the reservoir is drained and flushed with non-nutritive water.

The cloning reservoir is always maintained at 300 ppm. The mother plant is now fed less nitrogen in order to prepare it for cloning.

Day 56

On this day, the water is emptied from the blooming reservoir. The area is cleaned, and the water is replaced with proper pH- and ppm-balanced water. The next set of pre-bloomers is moved from the cloning room and into the blooming area. The blooming area now holds 30 plants.

The pre-blooming area, now void of plants, has its reservoir drained and the entire area is cleaned. Fresh water is returned to the reservoir and the pH and ppm are balanced to the proper readings. The fresh-rooted clones are then placed into the reservoir. The cloning area receives a fresh tray, water and nutrients. The mother plant is cloned and her standard feeding is supplemented with a bit more nitrogen.

Day 63

When a weekly schedule is used, this is the day the water is changed in the reservoirs and fresh nutrients are applied. The nitrogen content in the feeding of the mother plant is lowered and the mamma is spray-misted more often.

Day 70

This is, of course, the day when all reservoirs are drained and the areas are all cleaned. The reservoirs are replenished with fresh water and the pH and ppm levels are balanced. Clones are created and the mothers are fed more nitrogen. All standard procedures are followed.

The schedule is routine. The fourth set of pre-bloomers is placed into the blooming area. The first plants are moved from the pre-blooming area, where they have been for six weeks, to the blooming area. They are only two weeks from being in full bloom.

There are now two ways to proceed. Some gardeners continue to grow the almost ready-to-harvest plants in the standard hydroponic grow bed. Others use the wick method for the last two weeks of the blooming process for the 10 most advanced plants. In this case, the plants are removed from the hydroponic grow area and are placed in the standard wick method configuration (see Chapter 9). This method configures to a 40-plant blooming area so that space for 30 plants is sectioned off for hydroponics and space for 10 plants is set aside for the wick method.

Day 84

Today all standard operations continue in the cloning and blooming areas. However, this day is the first harvest of 10 bulbous 18-to-22-inch mega-buds. Harvesting repeats every 14 days.

Glossary

Acid—Opposite of alkaline; the lower part of the pH scale (1 to 6).

Air—A gaseous mixture that is mostly nitrogen and oxygen. Because air is a particle-carrying medium, it must be constantly circulated.

Alkaline—Opposite of acid; the upper part of the pH scale (8 to 14).

Apical Meristem—The uppermost growing terminal of a plant.

Artificial Light—Special lighting equipment for growing plants.

Backflow—The ability of water to flow backwards through the device (such as a pump) from which it came.

Ballast—The starter and regulator of electricity for artificial lights.

Bone Meal—An organic nutrient used for flowering plants.

Bonsai—A pruning technique to create properly shaped plants.

Branches—Lateral growth terminals at the nodes of a plant.

Breathe—Plants "breathe" different portions of the same air humans breathe.

Bud—A small protrusion on a stem or branch that can contain an undeveloped shoot, leaf or flower.

Calcium—Hard metallic element that serves as a secondary nutrient.

Capillary Action—An interaction between a solid material (i.e., wick) and a liquid (water) that causes the liquid to be drawn in a particular direction.

Carbohydrates—A group of organic compounds produced by photosynthetic plants that act as a major energy source in the diet and are crucial for root growth.

Carbon Dioxide (CO_2)—A gas that is an essential ingredient for all plant life.

Catalyst—A substance that helps increase the rate of a reaction.

Chlorophyll—A group of pigments found in photosynthetic plants that gives marijuana its green color.

Clones—The part of a single plant that is removed and used to begin a new plant that will be produced asexually.

Copper—A trace element used as a nutrient.

Cotyledon—A leaf of the embryo of a seed plant which appears from a germinated seed.

Decarboxylation—The slow removal of certain atoms (the carboxyl group) which precipitates the production of psychoactive chemicals.

Drain—The overflow or backflow tube in a grow bed.

Ebb and Flow—Hydroponic process that delivers water periodically to the roots of plants.

Epsom Salts—A source of hydrated magnesium and sulfate.

Exhaust—The exit of air from a grow room.

Female—The sinsemilla-producing gender of marijuana plant.

Fertilize—To make soil more fertile by spreading substances into it designed to increase its capacity to support growth.

Fertilizer—Synthetic and organic materials (including manure as well as nitrogen, phosphorus and potassium compounds) used to fertilize the soil.

Film/Flow Technique—The nutrient flow/film method of hydroponic growing that uses a constant flow of nutrient water. See: NFT.

Flooding—Filling a container with water to submerge the roots of the plants.

Flowering—Forcing plants to bloom by reducing their light cycles.

Fluorescent—Type of lighting tubes best suited for seedlings and clones.

Foliar Feeding—Spraying nutrients directly on the leaves of plants to feed them.

Genetics—The study of heredity and the manner in which characteristics are transmitted to related organisms via seeds.

Germination—The coming into existence of a plant from the seed.

Guano—Bird and/or bat excrement used as a fertilizer.

Harvest—The process of gathering a marijuana crop for drying.

HID—High-intensity discharge lighting (those big bright lights).

Hormones—Chemicals that stimulate growth and regulate development, such as rooting hormones.

Humidity—Relative moisture in the atmosphere.

Hydroponics—A technique for growing marijuana in the absence of soil using inert media with water/nutrient delivery systems.

Insecticide—See: Pyrethrum.

Iron—A trace element used as a nutrient.

Irrigation—Flooding an area with water on a timed schedule.

Lava Rock—Porous clay-type water holding hydroponic medium.

Light Rail—A device (also called a balancer) that moves the light fixture and distributes the light more evenly to the plants.

Lime—Various mineral and industrial forms of calcium oxide used as a pH stabilizer.

Macro-nutrients—Secondary nutrients such as calcium and magnesium.

Magnesium—A secondary nutrient.

Male—The less desirable gender of marijuana plant.

Mamma—A term used to describe a mother plant from which clones are taken.

Manganese—A trace element.

Marijuana—The cannabis plant.

Mealy Bugs—White, oblong, scaly, 1/16"-long bugs that live in groups.

Medium—A non-nutritive substance used as a stratum in hydroponic growing.

Metal Halide—A powerful cloning area light that uses a chemical compound of a halogen.

Micro-nutrients—The trace elements, including boron (B), copper (Cu), iron (Fe), molybdenum (Mb), manganese (Mn), sulfur (S) and zinc (Zn).

Misting—The act of spraying plants with either plain water or nutrient reinforced water.

Mites—Small parasitic insects that are one of the most common plant infestations.

Molybdenum—A trace element.

Mother Plant—The mammas from which clones are taken.

Nutrient flow/Film (NFT)—A method of hydroponic growing in which uses a constant flow of nutrient water.

Nitrogen—First primary nutrient listed on fertilizer containers.

N-K-P—Nitrogen (N), potassium (K) and phosphorus (P): the three primary nutrients listed on fertilizer containers that are usually followed by a number indicating the percent of each nutrient in the formula.

Nodes—The axis along the stem where the leaf, leaf spur and branches appear and where male and female indicators emerge.

Nutrients—The 12 elements that plants use as food.

Overflow—A tube or hose that regulates the water level in the hydroponic grow bed.

Oxygen (O)—The element on which all life depends.

Passive—Technique of capillary action water movement.

Peat Containers—Small peat moss containers that are used in hydroponics.

Perlite—Heated sand that is used as a hydroponic medium.

Perpetual Harvest—Part of the Sea of Green method, in which the grower continually harvests the crop on a regularly scheduled, ongoing, never-ending basis.

Pesticides—Chemicals (only horticultural pyrethrum is recommended) used to kill insects.

pH—The measurement of acidity (1 to 6) or alkalinity (8 to 14); 7 is neutral.

pH Tester—Meter to determine correct pH.

Phosphorus (P)—A primary element that serves as a nutrient for the plants.

Photoperiod—The amount of time that determines the effect light has on a plant.

Photosynthesis—Chemical reaction within a plant between the plant and light.

Pistils—Two whitish hairs that protrude from the female bract.

Pollen—The male gene-bearing microspore.

Potassium (K)—Primary nutrient.

Pre-bloomers—The rooted clones that are growing to the optimum height prior to being transported to the blooming area.

Propane—Gas used to heat room or produce CO_2.

Pyrethrum—An insecticide made from dried flower heads of chrysanthemums that is the only organic insecticide suggested for use on marijuana.

Reservoir—The water-holding containers used in a hydroponic grow system.

Resin Glands—Small structures found mostly on female reproductive pods which hold psychoactive substances.

Root Growth Additives—Any number of additives that stimulate root growth, such as Ortho Starter™.

Roots—The part of a hydroponic plant that is held in a medium other than soil from which it draws minerals and water.

Sea of Green—A mass-production growing technique based on the manipulation of the photoperiod of clones so that they are grown rapidly and then forced into flowering and harvesting.

Secondary Nutrients—Calcium (Ca) and magnesium (Mg).

Seed—A structure that houses the embryo and carries the genetic makeup of the future plant.

Stomata—Tiny openings on the underside of the leaves through which gas and water vapor flow.

Sulfur (S)—A trace element.

Taproot—The main root.

Timers—Electrical devices that regulate the operation of various tools, such as pumps, lights, etc.

Transpire—To give off water as a vapor.

Transplant—To move a plant from one medium to another.

Vegetative State—Initial stage of growth prior to blooming.

Ventilation—The proper exchange of air in a grow area.

Vermiculite—Horticultural substance used as a medium in a hydroponic system.

Vitamin B1—Helpful in eliminating transplant shock and stimulating rapid root growth.

Whiteflies—Winged insect pests.

Wick—Nylon strapping used to promote capillary action that brings water from its source to the plant.

Wind—Moving air is simulated by the fans in an indoor grow setup to help make the plants strong.

Zinc (Zn)—A trace element.

Ronin Books for Independent Minds

TURN ON TUNE IN DROP OUT ....Leary TURNON 14.95 ___
Classic Timothy Leary at his peak!
THE HEALING MAGIC OF CANNABIS ....Potter/Joy HEAMAG 14.95 ___
Healing power of psychoactivity, tinctures, food, list of med conditions
PSYCHEDELICS ENCYCLOPEDIA .... Stafford PSYENC 38.95 ___
LSD, peyote, marijuana and hashish, mushrooms, MDA, DMT, yage, iboga, etc.
MARIJUANA LAW, 2ND EDITION ....Boire MARLAW 17.95 ___
Increase privacy protections and reduce exposure to arrest
CANNABIS ALCHEMY .... Gold CANALC 16.95 ___
Classic and modern techniques to enhance potency
ECSTASY: The MDMA Story ....Eisner ECSTAS 17.95 ___
Legal status, psychological and physical effects, chemical synthesis
LEGAL HIGHS ....Gottlieb LEGHIG 12.95 ___
An encyclopedia of relatively unknown legal psychoactive herbs & chemicals.
GROWING THE HALLUCINOGENS ....Grubber GROHAL 12.95 ___
How to cultivate and harvest legal psychoactive plants.
GROWING EXTRAORDINARY MJ .... Gottlieb GROEXT 12.95 ___
Ancient and mern methods
MARIJUANA BOTANY ....Clarke MARBOT 24.95 ___
Sexing, cultivation, THC production and peak potency, continued production
MARIJUANA CHEMISTRY .... Starks MARCHE 24.95 ___
Species, seeds, grafting, and cloning, growing techniques and essential oils
CULTIVATOR'S HANDBOOK OF MARIJ ....Drake CULMAR 24.95 ___
Land and light concerns, harvesting and curing, psycoactive tobacco
COOKING WITH CANNABIS ....Gottlieb COOCAN 12.95 ___
For the epicurean marijuana enthusiast
PASS THE TEST .... Potter/Orfali PASTES 16.95 ___
How tests work, legal issues, how to avoid false positives and beat test
DR. ATOMIC'S MARIJUANA MULTIPLIER ....Todd DRATOM 12.95 ___
Underground classic on kitchen chemistry for increasing potency
PEYOTE & OTHER PSYCHOACTIVE CACTI .... Gottlieb PEYOTE 12.95 ___
Cultivation, grafting, cloning, nutrients, extractions, glossary of alkaloids, suppliers
PSILOCYBIN PRODUCTION ....Gottlieb PSIPRO 12.95 ___
Species, spore prints, culture techniques, harvesting, extraction, suppliers

Books prices: **SUBTOTAL** $_____

CALIF customers add sales tax 8.75% _____

BASIC SHIPPING: (All orders) **$6.00**

SHIPPING: add USA+$1/bk, Canada+$3/bk, Europe+$7/bk, Pacific+$10/bk _____

Books + Tax + Basic + Shipping: TOTAL $_____

Checks payable to **Ronin**

MC _ Visa _ Exp date __ - __ card #: _

Phone # (Req for CC orders)_ _ _ _ _ _ _ _ _ _ _ _ _ _ _ Signature_ _ _ _ _ _ _ _ _ _ _ _ _ _ _

Name_ _

Address _ City _ _ _ _ _ _ _ _ _ _ _ _ _ State _ _ _ ZIP _ _ _ _ _

Ronin Publishing, Inc.

Box 22900, Oakland, CA 94609 • Ph: 800/858-2665 • Fax: 510/420-3672
roninpub.com • Call for free catalog • Prices subject to change without notice